*To Mama and* ⟨...⟩
*gift for special* ⟨...⟩
*From Susan and* ⟨...⟩
*and Peanut.*

# A DOG
# AT THE
# MASTER'S
# TABLE

*Kim Tipton Brewer*
*and Belinda Belle Brewer*

By Kim Tipton Brewer

And

Belinda Belle Brewer, The Dog

Copyright © 2013 Kim Tipton Brewer
All rights reserved.

ISBN: 1492921491
ISBN 13: 9781492921493

Library of Congress Control Number: 2013920635
CreateSpace Independent Publishing Platform
North Charleston, South Carolina

# ACKNOWLEDGEMENTS

Belinda and I would like to thank all our Facebook friends who have so lovingly followed her page. You have blessed our lives with your friendship and encouragement. This book would not have been possible without you.

We would also like to give all our thanks and praise to the Lord, without whom nothing would be possible.

# FOREWORD

It MAKES ME SO happy to haves you here to feast on the good words of the book of Psalms with me! If you are a follower of my little Facebook page, then you already knows me. If not, I am a fourteen-year-old Yorkie girl named Belinda. I feels I haves lived long enough to learn a thing or two bouts life, bouts faith, and bouts God. The Lord haves issued all of us an invitation to taste hims words and learn of him. We will be talkin bouts things like facin the future with hope, dealin with illness and growin older, livin fearlessly in a scary world, handlin disappointment, and many other subjects regardin circumstances we encounters in life.

I must warns you that I haves little education. I haves never even beens to obedience school, so I uses bad grammar sometimes. Well, most of the time. But I feels I haves important life lessons to share because in my long life I haves experienced many of the trials that you humans face. We are goin to apply the truth of God's word to these situations. The book of Psalms is one of the tastiest books in the whole Bible and I wants us to dig deep enough to find hope, strength, and victory.

I thinks I hears the dinner bell ringin! Let's go in and sit at the Master's table.

# SATISFIED WITH GOODNESS

*"For he satisfieth the longing soul,*
*and filleth the hungry soul with goodness."*
PSALM 107:9

Haves you ever eaten somethin that just didn't satisfy? Haves you ever beens hungry for somethin you couldn't even name and tries many foods that didn't fill you up? At night I occasionally paces round and round my dinner bowl, pokin at it with my foot and whinin because I knows that I wants somethin but I doesn't knows what I wants. All I knows is that I am hungry for somethin that satisfies.

Lots of us are hungry for somethin that satisfies the deepest needs of our souls but much of what passes for spiritual food leaves us feelin emptier than ever. We mights be able to get by on a superficial feel-good gospel diet in the good times when everybody is in good health, the bills are all paid, and we are gettin along great with our family members. That is the marshmallow fluff kind of food. It's okay as an occasional treat but it won't fill us up when life gets messy. It won't satisfy our hunger when somebody is sick, or when a spouse walks away, or when the pink slip comes and we can't pay the mortgage. For those times we needs a diet that fills up the empty spaces in our souls and satisfies our longin hearts. As an East Tennysee girl I cans tell you that in the hard times we needs to put the spiritual soup beans and fried taters on the table. It's time to bake up a good hot skillet of corn bread and slather on the sweet cream butter of truth. It's the kind of situation when we haves to dig deep into the cobbler of stick-to-your-ribs scripture.

The Bibles in my house show the most wear on the pages of the book of Psalms. There are one hundred and fifty of these inspired songs to feeds the hungry soul, and while time and space won't permit taste-testin them all, we will feast on some mighty fine treats, spiced up with a sprinkle of other scripture here and there. I haves yet to meet any trial or any praiseworthy occurrence that there isn't a psalm to match. Because I haves reached somethin like a mature ninety-two years in dog years, I haves learned that life is easier to handle when we applies scripture to it, so I asks you to come along with me on a progressive dinner through the book of Psalms where we will sample dishes for every occasion.

This world sometimes feels like a land of heavy and back-breakin labor under a scorchin sun but we haves a God who knows this. Him understands our hunger and thirst and him haves provided a buffet for the famished soul and cool sweet water for the thirsty heart. Let's sit down at the Master's table and allow our God to feed us.

*"I am the Lord thy God, which brought thee out of the land of Egypt:*
*open thy mouth wide, and I will fill it."*
PSALM 81:10

# HOPE CONTINUALLY

*"But I will hope continually, and will yet praise thee more and more."*
PSALM 71:14

THE PSALMIST IS IN a worried state of mind and is surrounded by troubles but him haves determined in hims heart to hope in God. Him believes God loves him and haves good plans for him. Him is lookin at these troubles as a temporary thing because him trusts that God is faithful and will rescue him.

We never knows what we might haves to face in life but it seems like we cans get through anything as long as we haves hope. Hope gives us strength to get up in the mornin to do what we needs to do even when we feels like givin up. Hope whispers to us that even though today looks bleak, tomorrow mights bring the change we beens prayin for. Hope makes us believe a job is on the way when we haves unpaid bills. It puts power in our legs so we cans walk away from a loved one's grave. It gives peace when we gets bad news bouts our health.

# A Dog At The Master's Table

I thinks loss of hope is the main reason some folkses commit suicide. If you haves suffered the loss of a loved one due to suicide my little heart goes out to you. If you haves been left behind by someone who took their own life you may be dealin with hurt, anger, intense grief or even feelins of guilt because you didn't know that person hads lost hope and lost their way. I haves great compassion for the pain they felt and for the pain they caused. I believes that life became too hard for them when they lost hope. And if you are the person who sometimes feels like life is not worth livin anymore, let me pull out a chair for you at the Master's table. You are always welcome here. Him haves words of hope for you.

It seems to me that the key to survivin our problems is to not lose hold of hope even when everything around us looks dark. We must haves the faith to believe that things will get better even when it seems impossible. We can't always see the thing we are hopin for and that is wheres our faith comes in. We haves to believe that better days are up ahead around the bend.

Sometimes when I goes on a walk I almost gives up right before we gets back to the house. Just past my house there's a curve and then a dead-end road that turns to the left. It's a great place for walkin because there is practically no traffic at all. As I am ploddin along and lookin down at the ground I sometimes forgets how close to home I am and I lie down in the road and refuse to move. My house with a big cold bowl of water is right up ahead around the curve but I can't see it and I stops believin in it. Just because I can't see it doesn't mean it isn't there. That must be why Romans 8:24 tells us, "For we are saved by hope: but hope that is seen is not hope: for what a man seeth, why doth he yet hope for?" Believin in what we cans see doesn't exercise our hope at all and it sure won't put any faith-muscle on our bones. Hope is the thing that tells us not to give up when we feels we haves every reason to give up, because hope knows somethin good is around the bend.

# HOPE CONTINUALLY

I enjoys goin with my humans to our local drive-in theater and I haves noticed a funny thing happenin there. There are always a certain amount of people who leaves the drive-in durin the last five minutes of the movie so they doesn't haves to wait in line to get out. It's a puzzlement to me, especially when I sees they haves very young kids with them, because they never sees the endin to anything. It mights be makin the children think that no story haves a happy endin. The last five minutes of the movie is when the detective catches the bad guy or when the hero gets the girl. If we drives off before any of that happens then we are left with the image of the girl still tied to the train tracks and no rescuer in sight. I wonders how many times in life we gives up and loses hope when a happy endin weres, figuratively speakin, just five minutes away.

How cans we get some of this soul-sustainin sustenance called hope? One of the best ways is to read what God says bouts himself and bouts how much him loves us and what hims goin to do for us if we trust him. We needs to gets us a good Bible and spend time readin it every day. There are all kinds of study Bibles, concordances, and websites that cans help us find passages dealin with whatever need or problem we haves. Studyin the words of truth is like eatin a well-balanced meal before startin a busy day. It's good solid food like those soup beans and fried taters I mentioned earlier. It keeps our hearts steady and our faith solid as we waits for God to act on our behalf. As the psalmist says in 130:5, "in his word do I hope." His word gives us somethin dependable to hold onto while we waits for a happy change in our circumstances.

There haves been times in my own household or in our circle of family or friends where nothin we coulds actually see or feel showed any promise of hope but we trusted in a God who is able to do all things. We didn't put our hope in man but in a God for whom nothin is impossible. Some of these problems went on for years with no solution in sight, but we pressed on until God stepped in. There are still people we are prayin for and issues we are prayin bouts but we believes God is faithful and that him is mighty to save.

You mights be thinkin to yourself, "Now, Belinda, you probably hasn't ever seens or heards of the kind of problems that are goin on in my life." Without betrayin the privacy of any friends or family members, I assures you that I haves most likely seens or heards of the type of problems you haves, and nothin bouts your circumstances cans shock me. No matter how horrifyin, painful, or sordid your troubles are, I won't be shocked. After spendin fourteen years on this earth and livin closely with humans, I haves seens most everything and it coulds be that some of *my* stories woulds shock *you*. Unexpected and painful events come against us all. These events are sometimes of our own makin and sometimes they are the result of the bad choices of others. Either way, we ends up with unwanted chapters in the story of our lives. These are chapters we would haves done anything to leave out, chapters that broke our hearts and nearly broke our spirits, chapters that left deep scars and caused us to almost lose hope that things woulds ever get better.

There comes a day in all of our lives when we faces situations that look hopeless. One example most of us are familiar with is when a loved one gets diagnosed with a terminal disease and we knows there's no hope for recovery, short of a miracle. And sometimes God *does* lay hims hand on our loved one and him heals them against all the odds. But most of us haves hads to say goodbye to someone we loved very much when they didn't receive healin. My littermate sister, Bonnie, passed away in July 2011 when hers kidneys failed after a two-year struggle with Cushing's Disease and Diabetes. My humans and I hads prayed for those whole two years that those diseases wouldn't shorten hers life but her lost the battle at the age of twelve. My own life and everything bouts it changed drastically with the loss of Bonnie and I grieved for a long time. We hads been together since birth and I never knew a day of livin without Bonnie. Now, over two years later, I haves adjusted for the most part, and I hopes to see her again someday.

I doesn't intend to gets dogmatic bouts this issue but I personally believes there is a place in heaven for animals too. The eighth chapter of the book of Romans explains to us that the entire creation waits for redemption, for the day when men and women are redeemed and elevated to their position of the sons and daughters of God, because the creation itself will be set free from disease and death. I doesn't know if this is talkin bouts animals in heaven, or just animals on earth, but I knows that God is fair in whatever him does. In my own little heart I haves faith that God will restore and renew everything him mades. The Bible isn't absolutely clear on the issue of animals in heaven but one thing I cans be sure of is that 1 Corinthians 2:9 says, "But as it is written, eye hath not seen, nor ear heard, neither have entered into the heart of man, the things which God hath prepared for them that love him." This means there are things in heaven we hasn't even dreamed of! Those things coulds very well include animals.

I also believes humans haves an eternal soul and that death is just a transition from one type of life to the next. It's like goin through a doorway into another room. It isn't the end of humans when the door on this life closes and the Bible gives us comfortin words bouts those in Christ who haves gone on ahead. Here's what the Apostle Paul hads to say bouts this subject in 1 Thessalonians 4:13,14: "But I would not have you to be ignorant, brethren, concerning them which are asleep, that ye sorrow not, even as others which have no hope. For if we believe that

Jesus died and rose again, even so them also which sleep in Jesus will God bring with him."

You haves hope of seein your loved ones again. You doesn't need to despair. Our God haves mades a way for you to go be with him after this life and to see those who haves gone on before. We will gets deeper into this subject later on, durin our main course, but for now I wants you to think on a God who created us all, who loves us and knows each one of us personally, and who haves a plan for our lives here and for our lives after we leaves this world. We haves much to hope for, no matter what our circumstances are today.

I will shares a little story with you that Mommy shared with me. Her weres feelin real down and out several years back, and her weres drivin down the road in a depressed and hopeless state of mind when the followin verse from Psalm 42:5 came into hers mind: "Why art thou cast down, o my soul? And why art thou disquieted in me? Hope thou in God: for I shall yet praise him for the help of his countenance." Her weren't even sure at that moment where to finds this Bible verse but her suddenly felt like jumpin up and down for joy. This is a true sayin in the psalm, that the time will come when we will praise him again, no matter how we feels today. So now when we gets bad news in our household we says, "I will yet praise him." When we mades an emergency vet trip a few months back and didn't know if I weres gonna live or die, Mommy saids through hers tears, "No matter what happens, I will yet praise him." When the unexpected bills come or the car or an appliance breaks down we says, "I will yet praise him." When we are worried and cast down in spirit, even though we doesn't feel like sayin it, we says it anyway. So often we ends up praisin him far sooner than we expected.

# HOPE CONTINUALLY

So if you beens feelin hopeless I haves good news for you. It is temporary. No matter how long a certain situation haves been goin on, an end will come. There is hope. Somebody loves you. Somebody knows every thought in your head and every desire in your heart and every secret tear you ever cried. Him is on hims way. You will yet praise him.

# FORSAKE ME NOT·

*"Cast me not off in the time of old age;*
*forsake me not when my strength faileth."*
PSALM 71:9

GETTIN OLDER HAVES PREVENTED me from doin some things I used to really enjoy. Along bouts Christmas 2012 I stopped leapin onto the back of the sofa to watch the world from my favorite window. That old arthritis sneaked into my bones without my permission and against my will. As if I didn't already know how stiff and sore I am, I haves the x-rays to prove it. My corner of the kitchen countertop looks like a nightstand at the retirement home with its assortment of supplements and prescription pills. A quick glance at the bottles tells you I regularly takes senior-formula vitamins, glucosamine, fish oil, children's aspirins, liver pills, a prescription anti-inflammatory, three kinds of heart pills, a bronchial dilator, pills to help me go to the potty, and pills to keep me from goin to the potty too much.

# A Dog At The Master's Table

It's a delicate proposition at best to keep my system regulated on all fronts. Plus, haves anybody noticed how things don't taste the same as they did in our younger years? I used to enjoy practically any food and weres a wholehearted follower of the all you cans eat diet. It didn't matter if it weres on my plate or somebody else's; I tried my best to snap it up. Now it seems like things all taste the same.

Good eyesight is another thing of the past. Some old unwelcome fellows called cataracts haves taken up residence in both eyeballs. It used to be I coulds see a rabbit at fifty paces; now I feels lucky to see him pass by my nose. I suppose it hardly matters since I can't chase him anymore anyway. Oh, sometimes I pretends like I'm goin to chase him, but it's really just for show. Our clay-dirt yard won't grow much nice grass so it's pretty much all clover and there are anywhere from one to three fat rabbits grazin out there at any given time. They looks slyly at me from the corners of their eyes, not movin, not even pretendin to be terrified at the very sight of my fierce terrier presence. I cans no longer send them scatterin in all directions with just a low scary growl.

As if the ailments of old age weren't embarrassin enough, I once mades a hasty trip to the vet to check out two large lumps which came to my notice just above my hip area. My humiliation reached never before imagined greatness when I weres diagnosed with "fat pockets". Who gave my youthful metabolism its walkin papers? I only eats two square meals a day, one dental bone, any crumbs I cans vacuum from the kitchen floor, and all the morsels I cans beg from my humans. Why, that's hardly any food at all! There once weres a time when I would haves been svelte and stylish on a diet like that.

No longer cans I walk for long periods of time but must be pushed in my beautiful pink and green stroller. People sometimes stare at me in it as if they never saws a doggie wearin a dress and sittin in a stroller before. Not long ago I actually heards a man screamin out the window of hims truck, "There's a dog in a dress!" Him pointed at me and actually kind of embarrassed my daddy. Well, it's embarrassin for me too, havin to be pushed around like that, but what cans I do? I pass babies in strollers and even the babies look astonished at me. Some of the babies seem stricken with a case of envy when they sees all the features of my stroller. Mommy says it's kinda funny the way I checks out the baby strollers, and the way the babies checks out my stroller, but I'm not sure how funny it really is.

The infirmities of old age cans cause us to feel dependent and burdensome. Not bein able to guard the property or scare away the garbage men takes a hard swing at our pride. Those pesky fearless rabbits sit smug and fat as a constant reminder of our slow slide into decrepitude. We starts to wonder if we still seems useful to anybody. We feels afraid that we are in everybody's way. We chafes at our inability to be as vigorous and independent as we once weres.

While ponderin these depressin thoughts between naps, it occurred to me that a wise God haves our best interests at heart when him gradually takes away our sense of self-reliance and independence. As we approach our twilight years, we relearns the lessons of our early youth. We learns that we can't meet all our needs ourselves, that we needs someone stronger than ourselves to lean on, that we must live every day in complete dependence on and absolute trust in our God. As our image of ourselves as creatures of great strength and ability grows smaller, the vision of our mighty and omnipotent God grows larger as we learns that him is more than able to meet our every need from birth to death. After all, the older we gets, the closer we are to meetin him face to face, and the trials of our advancin years are helpin us to know him better in preparation for that day.

# A Dog At The Master's Table

The Lord is trustworthy from beginnin to end, in the strength of youth or the feebleness of great age. We cans trust him with the small things and the big things. If you haves trouble trustin him then I urges you to start talkin to him bouts every little thing. Nothin is too small to talk to God bouts. Doesn't you enjoy it when your children tells you all the details of their day? God is the same way! Him loves it when hims children takes time to sit down and tell him everything that's goin on in their lives. It doesn't matter that him already knows those things. Even though you mights be home with your small child all day, and you knows everything they dids, you still enjoys havin them come to you and talk bouts their adventures.

I am suggestin this exercise because I believes it really helps. Start by prayin for folkses you love or those you pass on your way to work. Pray for the safety of children when you drive by schools or pass the school bus on the road. Pray bouts doin your job today or bouts any other task you needs to accomplish. We lives in a busy world and it certainly cans make us feel frazzled and anxious, so prayin as we runs around doin errands is very helpful in calmin us down and keepin our minds on the Lord. Life seems less out of control when we focuses on the one who is in control of the whole world. As you learns to trust him in small things you will be able to bring bigger and bigger problems to him. The Lord Jesus saids this bouts trustworthy humans in Matthew 25:21, "His lord said unto him, well done, thou good and faithful servant: thou hast been faithful over a few things, I will make thee ruler over many things: enter thou into the joy of thy lord." Now, if the Lord Jesus says humans cans be trusted with big things if they are faithful in little things, how much more cans we trust God with big things because him is faithful in the little things?

From our first breath to our last, God haves hims eye on us. Him is more than able to care for our every need. My humans didn't have children and they are in theirs forties now. That means, in dog years, they are well over three hundred years old! It's far too late to do anything bouts the lack of children now. For the most part they are content with the way things are but one day I heards Daddy wonder aloud who will helps him and Mommy when they gets old. Here is the answer from the faithful one: "And even to your old age I am he; and even to hoar hairs I will carry you: I have made, and I will bear; even I will carry, and will deliver you." Isaiah 46:4

As we becomes smaller and weaker with age, we needs to let God become bigger and stronger in our minds and hearts. Him haves mades us and him will carry us.

# DESIRES OF THINE HEART

*"Trust in the Lord, and do good; so shalt thou dwell in the land, and verily thou shalt be fed. Delight thyself also in the Lord: and he shall give thee the desires of thine heart. Commit thy way unto the Lord; trust also in him; and he shall bring it to pass."*
PSALM 37:3-5

LIKE PRETTY MUCH ALL the promises of the Bible, this promise of givin us the desires of the heart comes with conditions attached. First we must trust in the Lord. It woulds be difficult to come to him with the desires of our heart if we didn't believe that him is there and that him wants to help us. We must also do good, which means livin a life that pleases God and livin a life that shows kindness to others. The Lord Jesus saids that the two greatest commandments are to love God above all else and to love our neighbors as ourselves. If we love God we naturally want to do the things that please and honor him. If we love our neighbors we naturally want to treat them as we woulds want them to treat us.

# A Dog At The Master's Table

The next thing we must do is delight ourselves in the Lord. For example, I knows that my humans are delighted in me because of the way they always considers my feelins and my comfort, and because of the way they enjoys showin love and kindness toward me. When we are delighted with someone we wants to spend time with them and know more bouts them. We wants to please them in everything we do. This is how we knows if we are delighted in the Lord.

We also needs to commit our way to the Lord. We cans commit our work, our relationships, our way of livin, and our daily activities to his honor and glory, and therefore we are commitin our way to him and then him will bring to pass everything we need, includin any desire that he himself haves placed within our hearts.

We all haves desires of the heart. It's natural for us to haves goals for our lives. God mades us this way and him haves given us simple instructions on how to go bouts gettin the desires of our hearts met.

I often wants things that aren't good for me, like a second supper. Or I wants to pull all the stuffin out of my squeaker toys and eat it. These things are not good for me even though I wants them, so I thinks the first thing we shoulds do is evaluate whether the desires of our hearts line up with what we know bouts God and what hims word says. There are some things we wants that we know isn't good for us and if we are honest with ourselves, those things aren't in God's will for our lives. There is nothin wrong with many of the things we desire for our lives and God haves given us talents that should be used and needs that haves to be met. If the thing we desire cans stand up against the word of God, that is half the battle won, because if it's somethin that's good, and that lines up with what we knows bouts God, we cans then go ahead and start prayin bouts it with confidence.

I am goin to gives us some silly examples just to illustrate my point. Since we knows God haves saids in the ten commandments that we mustn't covet, it's no use prayin for him to gives you your neighbor's house, or hims wife, or hims nice car. God already saids we can't have that so we haves no problem understandin this is not in hims will for us. God is not goin to gives you your neighbor's wife. You mights be able to go over there and take her away from hers husband, but you will be doin it without God's blessin. However, there is nothin I cans see that is wrong with prayin for your own house or wife or car, as long as you doesn't value those things above your love and relationship with the Lord.

I often asks for an extra treat in the afternoon, even though I knows I'm on a diet to fight these fat pockets, and I'm not very surprised when Mommy says no. I am just checkin to see if her haves changed hers mind. Sometimes we treats the Lord that way. We knows him haves said somethin is wrong for us but we won't let go of wantin the thing, so every now and then we kinda pops our heads through heaven's door and checks to see if him haves changed hims mind. It's best just to let those wrong desires go so the Lord cans bless us with what is good for us. We will be much happier with what him chooses for us anyway.

Suppose you are single and lonely and wants a wife or a husband. This is a normal goal to haves and there is nothin at all wrong with wantin to gets married. The Bible says in the book of Hebrews that marriage is honorable and it also says in the book of Proverbs that when you finds a wife you is findin a good thing. So since we knows marriage is founded by God for the benefit of men and women, we knows it's fine to go ahead and start prayin for him to sends the person who is the right one.

# A Dog At The Master's Table

Does you know that I am a married doggie? On April 20, 2013 I married my wonderful Bichon Frise husband, Cooper. If you woulds like to see how handsome him is, please go onto hims Facebook page called "Cooper, As In Gary Cooper". I warns you that him mights be the most handsome guy you ever saws! We found love in our senior years but it weres worth waitin for, so don't give up and settle for what you knows isn't right for you. I weres thirteen and him weres eleven when we met and fell in love. Him haves mades me very happy and it's so nice havin a companion for all of life's adventures. I couldn't haves asked for a better guy and it's so comfortin to know we are goin to grow old together. I never expected to finds love like this and hads never even dreamed bouts it, so I am happily surprised and blessed to haves Cooper in my life.

I thinks life woulds be borin if we never hads plans or dreams. Workin hard for your family is always an honorable thing if you are doin it to takes care of them, pay the bills, and keeps a roof over their heads and food in their tummies. I knows it's possible to be obsessed with work and if the marriage partner or children are sufferin due to somebody bein at work more than they needs to be, it's time to gets priorities in the correct order. Life is short and it's important to enjoy time with your spouse or go to your children's ballgames or dance recitals. One those moments are gone, they are gone. Balance is an important goal in all our lives. I believes God shoulds be the first one on the list, then the spouse, then the children, then work, then hobbies and other interests. If we puts God as the top priority in our lives then the other things will fall into their proper place much better.

While I doesn't believe desire for success shoulds be an overwhelmin desire in our hearts, hard honest work honors the Lord and if we does our best him will reward us. We mights never be wealthy but the

Lord is faithful to supply all our needs accordin to Philippians 4:19. And remember what God said to Cain when Cain gave an improper and lazy sacrifice? In Genesis 4:7 God says, "If thou doest well, shalt thou not be accepted?" If we does the best we cans, God will accept our labor, and him will reward the good work we haves done. God will always honor an honest worker. When we are unwillin to do dishonest things to get ahead, we mights never make it to the top of the corporate ladder, but God sees our honesty and in due time I believes with all my heart him will bless us for doin what's right. It sure does makes me happy when I does the things I'm supposed to do and my humans pet and praise me for it and reward me with a treat. They sees everything I do, whether I do it right or whether I do it wrong, and God is the same way. Him rewards an honest and obedient child the same way my humans reward me for doin what I know I'm supposed to do.

King David became very upset when him looked around and saws dishonest and evil people gettin ahead of honest and good people, and when him saws folkses bein wealthy and successful from doin wrong. It grieved David's heart because him knew it weres unfair for folkses to mistreat others and gain success from it. Him saids in Psalm 73:3, "For I was envious at the foolish, when I saw the prosperity of the wicked." A thing like that cans make us wonder why we bothers doin good when it seems like the bad folkses are havin all the luck. David felt that way too until him went to the temple and talked to the Lord bouts it. Then the Lord showed him that those folkses' success and prosperity are temporary at best, but the good work of honest folkses will be rewarded here in this life and also in heaven. No matter how much money and things evil people store up for themselves in this life, no amount of those things will give them peace of mind or peace with God. Doin right will lead to godly and satisfyin rewards and to the right kind of success in time.

# A Dog At The Master's Table

Let's take this little book of mine for example. Lots of people who write books imagine themselves becomin multi-millionaires, runnin round all over the country signin books and livin off royalties. Sometimes that happens but most of the time it doesn't. I doesn't haves any of those expectations. In my little doggie mind the only thing I desires is that somethin in this book helps somebody. If only one person reads this book and finds hope in the Lord and hope bouts theirs circumstances, then in my opinion it's a success. If readin this book mades you feel better then it's a success. If it mades you feel loved then it's a success. If you decided to learns more bouts the Lord or spend more time with him then it's a success. If you comes to know Jesus as your Savior it's more than a success, because the Bible says there is rejoicin in heaven over every single person who comes to Christ. This is the only kind of success I desires with this little book, that people are helped and that God is honored.

It's important to note that the Lord's idea of success isn't always the same as the world's idea of success. The world tells us to follow the money and to do whatever it takes to gets ahead. That cans lead us into many dishonest and hurtful situations. As 1 Timothy 6:9 puts it, "But they that will be rich fall into temptation and a snare, and into many foolish and hurtful lusts, which drown men in destruction and perdition." My understandin of what this is sayin is that those who follow after riches, and who conduct theirs lives in whatever way they haves to in order to becomes wealthy, are hurtin theirs own selves. I doesn't think it is sayin that if God himself haves blessed you with riches for doin right that you will fall into foolish and hurtful lusts. However, I thinks riches cans become a snare to any of us if we aren't careful.

Money is not the solution to unhappiness. If it weres then we wouldn't see all these stories in the news bouts celebrities bein so miserable. They goes through multiple marriages, check in and out of rehab, fall into illegal and dishonest practices, and sometimes even die of overdoses. They are tryin to fill up the empty spaces inside their hearts with everything but God and they haves the income to provide just bouts any substitutions for God that the world offers. If we doesn't haves a solid foundation in the word of God, and if we aren't followin him as obedient children, money cans tempt us with lots of hurtful things. I'm not sure it's ever good for any of us to be able to haves anything and everything we wants. Just as it isn't good for me to haves the six meals a day that I really wants, it isn't good for all the treasures and pleasurable experiences of the world to be available to us.

God's way is to follow what him says and him promises to always be with us, to rescue us, to provide for us, and to gives us peace of mind. Sometimes God actually does give us monetary prosperity but we mustn't let riches be our goal. Instead we needs to live the kind of life we cans be proud of and the kind of life that honors the Lord. David speaks in Psalm 73 of realizin that all the riches the wicked haves cans be destroyed in a single second of time, but the work that the good people do will continue forever.

If you haves dreams for your life the best thing you cans do is pray bouts them and let God lead you in the right direction. I keeps wantin to go in the wrong direction at my house. We beens stainin our deck for bouts the past month. It's a big deck with lots of tiny little spindle railins and it's takin forever. To be honest, I feels impatient with the whole thing by now. I keeps havin to go out the front door which means bein carried by Mommy because I doesn't like goin up and down steps. We goes into the yard and I does my business and then I runs to the deck and tries to go back inside that way. Mommy runs after me tellin me to stop but I ignores her. Sometimes the boards are still wet with stain, like they weres today, and that means goin into the bathroom and havin all four of my feets thoroughly washed. I sure does hates havin my feets washed. If only

I hads listened and gone back to the front door like Mommy told me! This is what happens to us sometimes in life when we tries to reach our goals in the wrong way. There will be consequences like havin our feets washed in the bathroom sink with soap and water. Our goals may be good and wholesome, such as me just needin to get back inside the house, but if we takes the wrong path on the way to our goals we cans be faced with somethin unpleasant. I ended up with soggy feets because I didn't do what I weres told.

I haves learned in my fourteen years on this earth that it's always best to do what's right. There is a reward when we follow our Master. Him says so himself in Psalm 31:23, "O love the Lord, all ye his saints: for the Lord preserveth the faithful, and plentifully rewardeth the proud doer."

# A MISCHIEVOUS DEVICE

*"For they intended evil against thee: they imagined a
mischievous device, which they are not able to perform."*
PSALM 21:11

IN THIS CASE THE psalmist is talkin bouts people imaginin evil stuffs against
the Lord and we will gets to that subject momentarily. But all of us who
lives on this earth know that people sometimes imagine evil stuffs against
us too. It's a sad fact that at times we encounters folkses who treat us
badly and on purpose. I'm not talkin bouts folkses who unintentionally
hurt our feelins; I'm talkin bouts the ones who do wrong towards us just
because they feels like it, or because they haves somethin to gain from
it. The psalmist calls it imaginin a mischievous device because they plot-
ted this wrong thing in their minds ahead of time and planned out how
they weres gonna do wrong. It brings to mind the term often used on the
courtroom TV shows: "malice aforethought". It's an intentional, premedi-
tated act that is performed to hurt someone else.

# A Dog At The Master's Table

We can't avoid these hurtful situations because we lives in a fallen world where people sometimes use their free will to do bad things. We gets hurt by those who haves problems of their own that they takes out on those around them. We gets hurt by those who plot against us in order to gets ahead at work. We even gets hurt at times by those with whom we haves very close relationships.

When these disappointin circumstances come upon us we haves a refuge in the Lord. We knows that Jesus understands our pain because him weres betrayed by hims close friend and disciple Judas who hads followed him for the three and a half years of hims ministry. Judas hads witnessed all the miracles yet still found it in hims heart to betray the Lord. I haves heards lots of speculation regardin the motivations of Judas but I doesn't feel we cans be certain why him chose to betray the Lord. All we knows for sure is that him weres followin the evil intentions in hims heart, because we knows that him hads arranged beforehand to betray Jesus. Him hads imagined a mischievous device.

No matter who haves betrayed us, whether it weres a known enemy or someone we dearly love, Jesus knows this kind of pain. Hims own family didn't even believe in him but actually came to Jerusalem to persuade him to go home with them and stop hims ministry. I woulds venture to guess that many of those who voted to crucify him hads witnessed some of the miracles him dids. Some of them may have eaten the bread and fishes him multiplied on the day him feds five thousand. After a brief skirmish in the garden of Gethsemane in which Peter swung hims sword at a soldier, the disciples fled when Jesus weres arrested. Only John stood near the court while Jesus weres bein tried and only John stood by him at the crucifixion. Peter followed at a distance after Jesus' arrest to see what woulds happen and ended up denyin him three times. Jesus knows what it's like to be hurt and betrayed by others, so we cans go to him with confidence that him understands and cans help us.

The psalmist here says that evil peoples weres imaginin doin somethin bad to the Lord. Now, it seems impossible to do anything to hurt the Lord, because he is the Lord. But does you know that the Lord told the nation of Israel in Zechariah 2:8 that whoever touched them weres touchin the apple of hims eye? Anyone who is a child of God cannot be hurt without it also hurtin God. Him won't ignore it. Who cans ignore a poke in the eye? If you haves ever beens poked in the eye with somethin then you knows it hurts. The first thing we does when somethin hurts our eye is put our hand (or paw) over it to protect and soothe it. That's what God is sayin here. It will never go unnoticed by him when someone deliberately sins against us and hurts us. Him will cover us with hims hand and soothe us until the time comes when him makes all things right.

Another way God haves been hurt is when him hads to watch hims own son be beaten, spit upon, mocked, and finally crucified. I cans just imagine how hims heart broke that day. Watchin a thing that that woulds be terrible for anyone, but cans you imagine watchin this happen to your own child? But Jesus willinly took this upon himself as hims part in the plan of salvation, so the Father endured it for our sake.

Our defender is mighty and he is fair, so we never haves to worry whether him sees what happens to us and whether him will make things right. My sister Bonnie and I used to pick on each other for no particular reason, yet our humans never let us get away with mistreatin each other. The humans always bought two identical toys for us, hopin we wouldn't be jealous of each other. But I wanted both toys and I woulds grab Bonnie's and put it underneath me while I played with my own toy. That allowed me to enjoy my own toy while preventin Bonnie from enjoyin hers. It seemed fine to me that I hads both of them. The humans didn't see it that way at all and they hads mercy on poor little Bonnie by takin the extra toy away from me and givin it back to her. Even though I weren't at all interested in the idea of fairness, the humans took control and mades things right. That's what God is goin to do at some point. It may seems like somebody is gettin away with treatin us badly, and it may seems like evil folkses just keep on doin evil without receivin any consequences, but God haves hims own way of evenin things out at the right time.

Bonnie often imagined mischievous devices against me. I loved to chew my toys on the couch while sittin in between the humans. Her weres always watchin for an opportunity to grab my toys. I woulds sometimes needs to go gets a drink of water and as soon as her saws me leave the room, her woulds grab my toy, jump off the couch, and throw my toy in the corner. By the time I came back to the couch her woulds be back on it, sittin there lookin all innocent, and my toy woulds be missin. After lookin all over the couch for it I woulds haves to go see which corner her put it in. Sometimes this mades me angry but the humans wouldn't let me bite Bonnie in retaliation. I really wanted to bite her but they saids it weres better for them to scold her than for me to pull out a mouthful of hers hair.

God tells us in Romans 12:19, "Vengeance is mine; I will repay, saith the Lord." It's not our job to straighten things out or repay the person for what they haves done to us. That is a job for our Father. Sometimes our problems with others seems unendurable because they haves treated us so horribly wrong, but if we retaliates we will be doin it in our anger and pain and not with clarity of mind and justice. That's why we needs to leave the matter of vengeance up to our Father. We cans count on God takin care of hims children, just like a good parent takes care of their child.

# A MISCHIEVOUS DEVICE

Why does God tell us not to take revenge for ourselves? I haves thought bouts this a lot and I thinks it's because God is the only one who cans take revenge without gettin hims hands dirty. God is a perfect judge. God created the laws of right and wrong, so when him passes judgment and sentences anyone, him remains completely righteous. God keeps hims holy character at all times. I doesn't think we cans take revenge on someone without it changin us for the worse. Our character suffers when we repays a wrong. That's why him tells us to step back and let him handle it. We will be changed and mades dirty by doin evil to folkses in return for the evil they dids to us. God doesn't want this. It's for our own good that him feels this way. God wants us to keeps our eyes and our faith focused on him and to keeps our hands clean.

The best thing we cans do when somebody hurts us is to pray for them. I knows it's a hard thing to do. Our hearts aren't always in it. The last thing I wanted to do was pray for Bonnie when her took toys away from me and hid them in corners, but I loved her and the prayin weres easier because of that. We doesn't always feel a lot of affection for the person who hurt us and certainly that cans make it harder to say those prayers. We needs to remember that someone with a desire to hurt others is just goin to keep on hurtin others unless they are changed somehow. Imagine how miserable they must feel inside from whatever is causin them to imagine a mischievous device. Wouldn't it be better for them to lets God heal them? Wouldn't it be better for us to lets God heal our own hearts and cleanse us of anger, hurt, and bitterness? At first we mights not really feel like prayin for somebody who hurt us, but we cans do it anyway, and then at some point our hearts will follow our minds and we will genuinely want to see the person mades better. Here is somethin to think bouts: what if we hads spent as much time prayin for folkses as we haves spent complainin bouts them? Maybe they would haves already changed by now!

# A Dog At The Master's Table

We doesn't wants to be like Jonah who weres angry that God forgave the people of Ninevah when they repented. Jonah still wanted to sees them punished for their past behavior so him sat down and pouted and felt sorry for himself. Jonah hads judged those people in hims heart and him hads found them guilty and him wanted God to sentence them for their wrongdoin, even though they weres sorry and hads changed their hearts. God tried to talk sense into Jonah in a plain and logical way but Jonah weres havin nothin to do with that. My own understandin of what God weres tryin to say is this: God is the lawgiver and ultimately him is the one who haves been sinned against. God is also the ultimate judge and whatever him says goes. Him is thrilled when somebody repents and asks him to makes their heart right and change them into kind and lovin people. That is a wonderful thing and we shoulds be happy. As for whatever wrong they dids to us, God haves hims own way of makin things even, and who knows but what him will bless us a hundredfold for what we suffered, especially if we haves love in our hearts toward the wrongdoer?

We cans learn a lot from David's example in 2 Samuel 16. There weres an angry man named Shemei who weres throwin rocks and dust at David and cursin him. One of David's men suggested goin over and cuttin off Shemei's head. David told him no and then went on to say this in verse twelve, "It may be that the Lord will look on mine affliction, and that the Lord will requite me good for his cursing this day." We needs to hand over the whole matter of the mischievous device to God, and hand the person over to God, and give him room to bless us. The more we show humble and godly character in the aftermath of our hurt, the more God cans bless us.

Now we will move on to the second half of our verse which haves beens a puzzlement to me in the past. It says they weres not able to perform the mischief they imagined. I cans understand them not bein able to perform mischief against God, but we all knows that quite often folkses actually perform whatever evil they thought up in their minds toward us, so I hads to chew on this verse for a while to figure out its meanin. It seems to me that the answer is found in Romans 8:28, "And we know that all things work together for good to them that love God, to them who are the called according to his purpose." Although some of the things that happen to us are not good in themselves, God is able to take those experiences and turn them into somethin that actually benefits us. Havin somebody tell lies about us is not a good thing, but God cans build our character by the way we handles a situation like that. Bein betrayed by a loved one is a terrible thing, but God is able to draw us into a closer and deeper relationship with him as we turns to him for comfort.

Often the things that seem bad at the time turn out to be huge blessins later on. Sometimes God allows somethin to be taken from us because him haves somethin better in store. Sometimes the trial we goes through is preparation for a huge blessin or opportunity on down the road. We doesn't always know the purpose of the trial at the time, but later on we cans look back and see how God used it in our lives. There also are trials for which we may never know the reason until we gets to heaven but we cans be certain that if we trusts God with the trial, and with its outcome, the mischievous device will never be able to fulfill its intended purpose.

Whether a person or the devil himself imagines a mischievous device against any of us, God is far more powerful than they are, and him cans use this hurtful event to make us stronger and better. After all, him says in Isaiah 54:17 that no weapon that is formed against us shall prosper. This is why I believes the psalmist saids the mischievous device were not able to be performed. It will not have its desired effect on us. Let evildoers imagine whatever they wants. Just keep on doin right and expect God to turn misfortune into fortune. Let them sharpen their weapons day and night and imagine mischief against the children of God, but those weapons will never be allowed to prosper.

# THOU ART WITH ME

*"Yea, though I walk through the valley of the shadow of death,*
*I will fear no evil: for thou art with me; thy rod and thy*
*staff they comfort me."*
PSALM 23:4

Earlier THIS YEAR I rodes a chairlift for the first time. I weres very far from the ground but does you thinks I felt fear? No, because I felt safe in Mommy's arms. I knew her hads hers arms tight around me and that nothin bad coulds happen to me. Even though the situation looked scary there weres nothin to fear because I trusted her to protect me.

This chairlift took me over a parking lot, then across a very busy road, then up and up and up! I weren't sure where it weres goin but then suddenly we arrived at the top of the mountain and I coulds see miles and miles of God's beautiful creation. As if this breathtakin view weren't enough reward for bravin the journey, the little store at the top of the mountain hads ice cream for sale!

# A DOG AT THE MASTER'S TABLE

Sometimes the trip in the chairlift of life looks scary. We doesn't like havin our feets so far off the ground. We starts to worry bouts goin splat on that big flat parkin lot underneath us. Then there are all those cars whizzin by on the road that woulds surely run over us if we falls. The steep climb up the mountain is an anxious trip because we can't see where are goin. Who knows what coulds be waitin for us at the top?

Not knowin what lies ahead often makes the bravest of us faint at heart. Our hands tremble and our knees shake. We fret and stop eatin and stop sleepin and start gettin ulcers and we just generally turn into a miserable mess. I haves to confess that, despite my fearless ride on the chairlift, I still am reduced to a quiverin ball of fur when I visits the vet. On those occasions it doesn't mean diddlysquat how tight Mommy is holdin me or how many times her assures me that nothin bad will happen there. My imagination presents me with all kinds of horror-filled visions. The vet office haves unpleasant antiseptic smells and scary-lookin instruments on the countertops. How cans I possibly know if they are goin to use some of those contraptions on me? Before I know what's happenin I falls into a full-fledged panic attack. Mommy keeps tellin me her won't leave me there but I can't hear her over my loud frantic breathin.

We wastes a lot of time worryin bouts things that never happen. Even if those horrors *are* waitin for us somewhere just around the corner, how woulds worryin be preventive? The Lord Jesus tells us in Matthew 6:34 not to worry. Wouldn't it be far better to spend our energy layin those fears down at hims feets? There is nothin at all constructive bouts worry; instead of buildin somethin up we are tearin our own lives down. The best thing I knows to do when somethin weighs heavy on the mind is to go to the one who holds all things together and hand that burden off to him.

# THOU ART WITH ME

All our prayers rise up to the God of heaven like a sweet-smellin incense from the altar. Psalm 141:2 says, "Let my prayer be set forth before thee as incense; and the lifting up of my hands as the evening sacrifice." I wants us to think on this for a minute. This verse doesn't say anything bouts it bein only our noble prayers for world peace, or our lofty prayers with fancy words, or our prayers on behalf of others bein a sweet smell to our Lord. It just says "my prayer". There are times when our prayers aren't pretty. We sometimes come into the Lord's presence and lay at hims feets the broken things: angry feelins toward others, the hurt somebody caused us, a spirit of unforgiveness, a negative attitude, intense anxiety, lack of faith. We mustn't be ashamed to admit these things to him; it's not like him doesn't know. How cans him heal if we don't hand over?

Many times my late sister Bonnie or I mades holes in our squeaky toys. The stuffin all fell out and we weres in danger of swallowin the loose squeaker and chokin to death. At those times we hads to let Mommy take the toys away from us and mend them. I admits we occasionally tried our best to hold onto them. We didn't realize her couldn't help if we didn't hand over. Woulds we go to the human doctor or worse yet, the vet, with an injury and not let them stitch it up? That woulds be one of the most useless trips I cans think of, and we woulds pay good money for nothin. Well, the Great Physician haves hims hand out for the broken thing! We just needs to hand it over. We might haves to hand it over more than once, the same way Bonnie and I kept snatchin our squeaky toys from Mommy while her weres sewin up the holes. We may be so troubled by somethin, or haves such a hard time forgivin somebody, or be strugglin so much with fear that we keeps snatchin the broken thing out of our healer's hand. How light we feels when we place the burden on hims nail-scarred palm and how heavy we feels when we takes it back a day or two later. It's of no benefit to us to keep takin back the broken thing because it haves become unfit for its intended purpose, the same way mine and Bonnie's toys hads become unfit. They were of no use to us until Mommy mended them. I knows that the deeper a circumstance haves cut our souls, the longer it takes to heal. Sometimes I thought we woulds never get our toys back because we hads mades such huge holes in them, but the truth is that holes that large take longer to mend. That's why every time we realizes we haves taken the broken thing from the only one who cans stitch it up, we needs to put it back. The day will dawn when we hands it over for good and we come away healed. I believes this, even though I knows of hurts that haven't yet beens healed, because nothin is too hard for God. We can't start believin the lie that we will never be healed.

It's in the bad times we needs to remember that God haves hims arms around us the whole time. Hims holdin on so tightly that there is nothin to fear. Just like my Mommy weres holdin and protectin me on the chairlift, God is holdin and protectin us, and our only job is to trust in him and enjoy the ride. Yes, sometimes the ground seems far away and we can't feel the earth under our feets. Sometimes it looks like there is danger in our path. But if we just trusts that God haves us, and that him knows the way, and that him haves a plan for whatever is waitin for us at the top, we cans haves joy in the journey instead of fear. Just like I rested in Mommy's arms on the way up the mountain, we cans all haves rest and a sense of joy on our journey.

Remember, to get to the top of the mountain, we haves to climb into that chairlift, trustin that God is gonna hold us all the way, and him haves a wonderful surprise for us at the top. I would haves never seen the view if I hadn't taken a step of faith. Do we want to miss the blessins because we are too afraid to trust God? Sure, we mights be able to stay safe if we stay on the ground, but we will never gets to the top of a mountain that way and we will never grow in faith and in our relationship with our Father. How cans we trust him in all circumstances if we never steps out in faith and depend on him to lift us up? Him wants to take us up high and show us the view. There is spiritual ice cream there.

# THOU HAST HEALED ME

*"O Lord my God, I cried unto thee, and thou hast healed me."*
PSALM 30:2

Serious illness is somethin nobody wants to experience. It mights be a chronic type or it mights come upon us suddenly. I think it's one of the things that tries our faith the most. When we feels ill in our body it affects everything bouts our life.

In April 2013 I went to the vet because of some eye and ear allergies, plus a little annoyin cough. The vet heards a wheeze in my chest and dids an x-ray that showed my liver weres greatly enlarged. Well, now I hads more problems than I thought! I went into the office thinking I weres gonna get some eyedrops and eardrops, maybe an antibiotic, and then I woulds be on my merry way. Now I hads blood tests runnin in a little machine and an ultrasound appointment with a bigger animal hospital. My blood work mades the vet and Mommy both very unhappy because my liver enzymes weres way out of whack and the vet started tossin out all kinds of scary words, includin the word nobody wants to hear: cancer.

# A Dog At The Master's Table

Life has a way of throwin us for a loop like this. We thinks we haves a minor problem and suddenly we haves a major problem we never expected. It cans shake up our whole world. I used to wonder how King David weres able to say he woulds "not be moved" or in other words "not be shaken". King David experienced much adversity in hims life yet him weres sayin nothin weres gonna shake him. But in the midst of my tryin time of illness I learned what him meant. We cans be shaken *up* while not bein shaken *from* our faith in God. Why wasn't David shaken? "For the king trusteth in the Lord, and through the mercy of the Most High he shall not be moved," Psalm 21:7. I admits when I weres listenin to all those scary words from the vet I felt shaken up, but dids I lose faith in my God to see me through no matter what? No, because hims always with me. Whether him decides to heal or take me home, hims goin to provide for me all the way.

After a misdiagnosis of Cushing's Disease and feelin like I weres gonna die from the meds for that, and after receivin severely abnormal ultrasound results, I weres told I most likely hads liver cancer and that nobody in this area woulds take the risk of doin a biopsy to make sure. If I wanted to travel to the University of Tennysee they coulds do a biopsy on a senior dog with an enlarged heart like mine. Well, Mommy and I weren't willin to take that risk just to maybe be told I hads an incurable disease. We decided to continue with the liver supplement and my other medications. The vet prescribed some pain meds as well and then I hads a terrible reaction to them and thought I weres dyin yet again. The vet started sayin more scary words, this time to do with Mommy maybe havin to make some hard decisions soon.

We informed my Facebook friends bouts the sad news and they overwhelmed us with love and support and prayers. They held a prayer service for me and for other sick friends that night. The outpourin of love and friendship blessed my heart beyond my ability to describe. I knew my God weres with me, and that my friends and family weres with me, and I hads joy in my troubles.

By the next day I felt quite a bit better and as the days went by I improved more and more. All my tests since the end of May haves shown that my liver enzymes are pretty much back to normal, to everyone's happy surprise. Since my illness I haves celebrated my fourteenth birthday and the vet saids if things keep goin so well I will probably be celebratin my fifteenth birthday next year! I knows it's the prayers of my friends and the power of God that mades me well. God isn't finished with me yet and my work here on this earth isn't done.

I wants to make it clear that I am not sayin God heals in all circumstances, or that if enough people pray for us him will takes the disease away and make us whole. We all know that sometimes him takes us home to heaven instead. We haves all said sincere prayers for those who did not end up bein healed. My sweet sister Bonnie weren't healed. My grandpa on Daddy's side weren't healed when him hads cancer but went home to heaven instead. We haves all been crushinly disappointed when our prayers for healin weren't answered the way we hoped. I can't promise healin and I can't explain why sometimes him heals and sometimes him calls home. But I cans tell you that I firmly believes him haves a purpose in whatever result him chooses. I cans tell you I trusts him to do what is best.

In this life we doesn't haves all the answers. We doesn't gets a voice from heaven explainin why God chooses to heal some and chooses to take others to be with him. The question is, do we trust him anyway? Cans we hand over to him all our pain and disappointment and bitterness and anger, believin that even when we don't understand, him haves a purpose for everything that happens? God loves us and understands how we feel, even when our feelins aren't pretty, and him mourns along with us. Remember how the Lord Jesus wept at the grave of Lazarus? I doesn't think him weres weepin for Lazarus but for the pain and anguish of Lazarus' loved ones.

I woulds never want to belittle anyone's grief and I knows many of us haves experienced terrible anguish either over our own illness or the illness and/or death of someone we dearly love. We haves been angry with God at times, and some haves even decided to turn from followin him, or not believe in him. As a little dog I confesses that I doesn't know why things are this way. Not even the most faithful preacher of the word of God haves the answers to all our questions. But again I turns back to the example of King David who lived many years in hidin and in fear for hims life, whose own children turned against him, who endured the illness and death of hims own little baby. Yet him weres able to say, "I will not be shaken".

We will all be shaken up at times, just as I am sure King David often weres, but we don't haves to be shaken from our faith in God. I needs to make it clear that I am not sayin, "Oh, your loved one died and I don't know why. Just trust God." That woulds be like slappin a band-aid on a cut that needs twenty stitches. I am talkin bouts developin a livin, breathin relationship with God so that we cans feel hims presence with us in our troubles. That is the kind of relationship King David hads with God and that is why him coulds still praise God even in the bad times. I am talkin bouts spendin time in scripture, prayin to God, thinkin bouts God, gettin to know him and realizin him gives us blessins along the way. Durin the worst times in my family we haves often felt the Lord's presence beside us in such a real way that it seemed like we coulds reach out and hold hims hand. That is what I'm talkin bouts, not a mental belief that

God is in control and haves a reason for all that happens, but a heart belief that him is real and him cares and hims gonna see us through. We needs a nitty-gritty, nuts-and-bolts practical application of faith in our lives before we cans say, "I will not be shaken".

# REMEMBER NOT

*"Remember not the sins of my youth, nor my transgressions: according to thy mercy remember thou me for thy goodness' sake, O Lord."*
PSALM 25:7

I CERTAINLY WERES A little stinker in my youth and some days I still takes on a diva attitude. So many times I haves disobeyed my humans, and I haves played mean tricks on my late sister, and I haves beens selfish and greedy. Daddy once saids I hit the Terrible Twos and then stayed there! Not only haves I openly disobeyed many times, but also I haves neglected to do the good things I know I needs to do.

Why haves I beens so mean at times? Well, because it's fun! Even the Bible says it's fun when it tells us that Moses decided to help the nation of Israel because of hims faith in God, "choosing rather to suffer affliction with the people of God, than to enjoy the pleasures of sin for a season", Hebrews 11:25. Doin wrong cans be lots of fun and Moses could haves stayed in Egypt and enjoyed all the treasures and wickedness there, but the second half of that verse is the important part. The fun only lasts for a short time and then comes the consequences.

Sometimes the consequences of my wrongdoin appear in the form of knowin how disappointed Mommy is with me, like the time I chewed the trim off the laundry room door, or the time I chewed the corner off the brand-new custom kitchen cabinets, or the time I pulled the curtains down and the curtain rod out of the wall, or the time I ate hers new sandals her weres gonna wear on vacation. Well, you gets the picture: I haves destroyed many items. At those moments I realized I hads done wrong, and as I sat there in the debris, I felt guilt. My head started hangin low and my tail started doin this weird thing where it tucked underneath me. I didn't want to feel that way or haves my tail wrapped down over my behind like that, but I couldn't help it. The gleeful tearin up of things that hads been so pleasurable just moments before weres now a testimony of shame. The only thing I coulds do weres slink up to Mommy and beg hers forgiveness. Oh the joy I felt when her smiled at me and petted my head and we weres best friends again!

Other times I received time-outs and the withholdin of rewards due to my transgressions. I liked to fight with Bonnie every time we started out the door for a walk. I wanted to go out the door first. As a result of bein mean to her, I often got held back by Mommy and I hads to watch Bonnie trot out ahead of me. Honestly, I really believes if Bonnie could haves stuck her tongue out at me her would haves. Sometimes both of us acted up so much while goin out the door that we hads to sit in time-out for a few minutes and then try again. There weres times we weres all bouts to go for a ride but Bonnie and fought so much that we got left home instead. That is the problem with doin wrong. Sometimes the con-sequences are very unpleasant and make the wrong thing not even worth it. It seems fun at the time but the punishment is no fun at all.

I often broke the commandment that says "thou shalt not steal". I tries to steal Bonnie's food at every meal. Mommy hads to stand over us at mealtimes so I couldn't take Bonnie's food. Boy, did Bonnie gets mad whenever I stole hers favorite red ladybug toy! I bets that even right this minute her is gloatin over the fact that hers ladybug toy is in hers urn with her.

Bonnie liked to pout and hold a grudge for a little while, no matter how much I licked her face after I dids somethin mean to her. She woulds show all her teeth and growl at me. She wouldn't kiss me back at all. We all knows people like this. They likes to pout and hold a grudge against us even though we are sorry we dids wrong. The only thing we cans do in that situation is apologize and ask for their forgiveness and then let God do the rest. God cans restore all relationships if all parties are willin to let him. Unfortunately, people sometimes resist him and refuse to forgive us, and in those cases we just haves to let go of it knowin we dids all we could. Refusin to forgive is contrary to the instructions of Ephesians 4:32 which says, "And be ye kind one to another, tenderhearted, forgiving one another, even as God for Christ's sake hath forgiven you." Because we ourselves haves received mercy, we haves no right to refuse mercy to others.

Every time Bonnie stole my chewy bones and hid them under the bed, I weres quick to forgive her. Even when her sometimes walked by me and decided to slap my face with hers paw for no reason whatsoever, I turned the other cheek. I haves always hads a cheerful and happy personality and I just can't stay angry. With the exception of the times I wanted to pull hers hair out for throwin my toys in the corner, I didn't hold grudges. I haves been forgiven of many bad things and so I can't refuse to forgive others.

# A Dog At The Master's Table

We knows we needs to forgive others but there are several reasons why we don't. One reason is that we thinks we are somehow punishin the person who hurt us by holdin a grudge against them. This is usually not the case because lots of times they doesn't even care, or even if they does, holdin a grudge can't change what haves already happened. Another reason we doesn't forgive is that it makes us feel like we are sayin it's okay that somebody hurt us. That isn't the case either because they are still accountable to God for what they dids to us. A third reason many of us finds it hard to forgive is because we just simply doesn't know how. But here is somethin I woulds like us to think bouts. Even though it's never God's will for someone to sin against us and hurt us, him is able to makes somethin beautiful of our lives as a result of our hardships. Him promises us in Isaiah 61:3 that him is able to gives us "beauty for ashes, the oil of joy for mourning, the garment of praise for the spirit of heaviness". Is anything worth missin out on the beautiful thing that God haves planned for us? No matter what somebody dids to us, or how tawdry it weres, or how evil it weres, that thing pales in comparison to the beauty the Lord haves in store for us. It's not even worthy to be compared to what him haves planned for our future. Don't let that person or that terrible thing keep you from pressin onward to your destiny and purpose in the Lord. Him is able to takes that hurtful thing and make your life somethin far more wonderful than it would haves been without it. Turn that hurt over to God and ask him to lead you on to whatever him haves planned to makes your life extraordinary. Holdin onto unforgiveness puts a barrier between us and the Lord's best blessins. It builds a wall between us and the beautiful thing him haves planned for our lives. I am tellin you we needs to step over that wall, or detour around it, or kick a hole in it and walk straight through it. Somethin beautiful is on the other side.

There is also the issue of us obtainin forgiveness for our own faults. It's very easy for little doggies like me to gets forgiveness from our masters. I knows how to make my big brown eyes look sad and I am so cute that nobody cans resist me. Humans fall for that every time. I must admit that makes it very nice for me when I haves been bad. You humans don't haves it so easy because, for one thing, you are not as cute as doggies. For another thing, you are not all sweet and helpless like a little doggie. So when it comes to obtainin forgiveness from your Master you really can't count on your looks like I can. Him knows you knows better and, since you are human, him haves to hold you to a higher standard. Him knows whether it weres a mistake you didn't know weres wrong or whether you dids it intentionally. Sometimes I haves been fooled into thinkin Mommy cans read my mind, but God really cans read the mind of humans and him knows whether you really are sorry or whether you are just pretendin the way I occasionally pretend to be sorry.

None of us is perfect, not even little doggies like me. If we weres able to do all things exactly right we wouldn't need to worry bouts forgiveness or bouts not livin in a way that honors the Lord. We haves already established that humans are not cute enough to get by on looks alone, but the good news is that God mades a plan for you to say you are sorry and to be forgiven by him.

Now, I realizes that I am talkin bouts life, forgiveness, and God from a Christian perspective and maybe not all my readers are of that particular faith, or maybe some readers don't profess a faith at this time. I wants you to know that I loves each of you exactly the same, whether you are a follower of any religion or whether you haves doubts bouts whether God is real and that him loves you. I believes God loves every person exactly the same and that it woulds be impossible for him to love you more than him already does, because him loves you to the fullest. God is the perfect kind of father, the kind everyone wants to have, and you cans know him just as well as you wants to know him. The invitation is open and constant. The best part is that you doesn't even haves to clean yourself up before goin to him. There are times when I gets really dirty havin fun and playin outside but when I goes to my humans they still pick me up and love me just as much as if I weres clean. It's their job to clean me up; I can't do it myself. God is the same way. Him invites you to come to him no matter what state you are in. It's hims job to clean you up. Him knows you can't do it yourself.

Right now we are gettin into the main course of our dinner at the Master's table. The main course often is the best part of the meal, but just in case dessert is your favorite part, we haves a wonderful treat in store for us a bit later on. At this moment I asks you to think on God, or on the possibility of God if you currently haves doubts. I am gonna lets you in on a little secret and I hopes you won't be shocked but even some of us who are the most devoted of believers haves moments of doubt. There are odd little instances where I thinks to myself bouts my beliefs, "This is crazy!" I guesses sometimes it all just seems too wonderful to be true. Sometimes the idea of such love is more than I cans imagine. If some of you are devout believers who haves never hads those sudden and momentary thoughts, that is a wonderful thing. I just wants to be honest with you that every now and then doubt comes skippin through my head wearin a scary grin and laughin in a creepy way. But then I looks around me at this beautiful world and all the things that are in it and I just can't imagine all of it bein an accident. That is what grounds me in faith every time: thinkin on the enormous universe we lives in, and all the people and all the creatures, even creatures no eye haves ever seens, and then I knows I believes somebody makes it all.

If somebody makes all things then I haves to assume him haves a purpose and a plan for each one of us. This is what the Lord saids in Jeremiah 1:5 when him called Jeremiah to speak to the nation of Israel:

"Before I formed thee in the belly I knew thee; and before thou camest forth out of the womb I sanctified thee, and I ordained thee a prophet unto the nations." So we sees that God hads plans for Jeremiah's life even before Jeremiah's mom weres expectin a baby! God knows us before we even exists here on earth and him haves plans for us, as him also says in Jeremiah 29:11: "For I know the thoughts I think toward you, saith the Lord, thoughts of peace and not of evil, to give you an expected end." We are in the thoughts of God at all times, and hims thoughts are good and are in our best interests. The God who mades us intends to gives us hope and a future. We are not on some dead-end road goin nowhere on a pointless journey. We mustn't give up and lie down in the road the way I sometimes does. We are on our way somewhere! We needs to press on and see what good things the Lord haves in store for us.

# DELIVER US

*"Help us, O God of our salvation, for the glory of thy name:*
*and deliver us, and purge away our sins, for thy name's sake,"*
PSALM 79:9

I KNOWS A LOT of really good people with big hearts. They cares deeply bouts the problems and needs of others, they supports charities, and they are the kind of friends who are trustworthy and kind. These sweet people belong to many different faiths and some of them are agnostic or atheist. I knows people of faith who are wonderful moral people and I knows people who don't profess any faith who also are wonderful moral people. All of them make mistakes just like I do. No matter how hard we try, none of us is perfect. The intentions of our hearts cans be of the very highest standards and still we make mistakes.

In the previous chapter we discussed the fact that as a cute little doggie, I am able to obtain absolution with these big brown eyes and puppy-like face and waggin tail. Humans, I am sorry to say, don't possess those qualities. The problem you face as humans is that you haves beens created by a holy God who expects holiness from you. However, your very human-ness gets in the way of perfection. So what is the solution? The solution is so simple it almost seems complicated: to be perfect for a perfect God you needs a perfect God to makes you perfect! It takes somebody perfect to make somebody else perfect. I can't make you perfect because I falls way short of the mark, and you can't make me perfect because you haves mades mistakes too. And goodness knows, we can't make ourselves perfect if we isn't perfect in the first place.

I confesses to you that I doesn't haves it in me to keep from failin at doin right, and you might as well go ahead and confess it too. We haves all messed up. We haves all told lies, or been disobedient and disrespectful, or stolen somethin, or hurt someone else, or wanted to see somethin bad happen to somebody, or beens jealous, or behaved dishonestly in work or business, and on and on. You gets the point. I personally haves committed several of those sins I just named and many more. Honestly, I woulds be ashamed to sit here and name all my faults. And when it comes to my humans, they haves committed more faults than I haves toes to count on. My humans woulds probably dig a big hole, crawl in it, and never come out if I told you everything they haves done wrong. Neither I nor my humans cans point a finger at anyone because we haves mades bad mistakes of our own. We are no better than anyone else and we haves fallen flat on our faces into the mud holes of error many times. The Lord called us to him by grace the same way him calls everyone else. If you sees anything good in us then you cans be sure it's the Lord you are seein.

Since we haves already established that you humans can't clean your own selves up, and as a doggie I doesn't needs to clean myself up, we are gonna concentrate on what to do bouts the human problem. The animal kingdom didn't fall from the grace of God and therefore doggies like me and all the other animals don't need redemption. It weres man who fell from grace and it still is man who needs a way to gets back into a right relationship with our maker. There is good news for you. Because you are imperfect and can't make yourselves perfect, God himself came down to this world to offer hims own self as the perfect solution for imperfect humans.

Just think bouts how much him loves you! Imagine the God who created every atom and every speck of dust in the entire universe lovin you that much! Him doesn't needs a thing from any of us, so I cans assure you it weren't out of need that him came runnin to the rescue. I cans just picture him lookin down from heaven with hims heart heavy in grief over all the hurt humans weres causin their own selves and others by makin mistakes. There weres no answer to be found, nobody in the whole earth who coulds come to your rescue. Nobody coulds do this God-sized job but him. As the prophet Isaiah says in Isaiah 59:16, "He saw that there was no man, and wondered that there was no intercessor: therefore his arm brought salvation unto him; and his righteousness, it sustained him." Nobody in all of heaven or earth weres man enough for the job but the Lord Almighty, so him dids the only thing him coulds do. "Then said I, Lo, I come: in the volume of the book it is written of me," Psalm 40:7. Who is the psalmist talkin bouts here? It's none other than the Lord Jesus Christ, accordin to Hebrews 10:7, which states that the fulfillment of this verse is found in Jesus himself.

There weres no intercessor to make peace between you humans and God, so God became that intercessor. This called for somebody holy and perfect to takes your place. The sentence for all sin, any sin, is death. God didn't want you to die and be separated from him because him loves you with all hims heart. Him grieved for you like a father grievin for hims lost children. There weres nothin else to do but come in the flesh and take your punishment on himself. God knew you needed a deliverer and so him became your deliverer.

The nation of Israel weres given the sacrificial system because, accordin to Hebrews 9:22, "And almost all things are by the law purged with blood; and without shedding of blood is no remission." As difficult as it may be for us to thinks of, as animals and animal-lovers, sin called for the death of the one who had committed it, but since God allowed animal substitution, the nation of Israel adhered to the sacrificial system in order to obtain forgiveness of sins. Today, thankfully, we doesn't haves to do that anymore because of the sacrifice that God himself mades once for all time. I doesn't wants to dwell on the aspect of animal sacrifice for long, so I'm goin to trust that God haves a fair and righteous plan and purpose for those animals and leave it at that.

Eventually the day arrived when God came here in the form of a man, in the flesh, to take your place. The Apostle John, who both saw the Lord Jesus Christ in the flesh before and after hims death on the cross, haves this to say bouts God's amazin rescue, "And the word was made flesh, and dwelt among us, (and we beheld his glory, the glory as of the only begotten of the Father,) full of grace and truth," John 1:14

John, of all the disciples, just may be the most qualified to teach us on the subject of God in the flesh, and how much you needs him. John lived, ate, and traveled with Jesus durin the years of hims ministry. John saw with hims own eyes the miracles: multiplyin of the food to feed thousands, healin of the sick, raisin the dead. John weres the only disciple who watched Jesus die the excruciatin and humiliatin death on the cross. John weres the first to believe in a miracle when him saws the empty tomb. John saws the risen Lord Jesus and again weres able to actually touch him and eat with him. Many years later, while exiled to the Isle of

Patmos for hims faith, John saws the risen Lord Jesus one more time, in all hims kingly and priestly glory. And John "fell at his feet as dead," Revelation 1:17

John isn't the only one who fell over like a dead man when him saws the glory of the Lord. Ezekiel, the prophet of God, also says in Ezekiel 1:28, "And when I saw it, I fell upon my face." Daniel, that godly and faithful man, also fell upon hims face when the Lord's angel Gabriel weres speakin with him, and him says in Daniel 8:17, "I was afraid, and fell upon my face". So we sees that even the glory of an angel weres too much for Daniel. In Acts 7:32 we are told that Moses, that great miracle worker and follower of God, says this when him saws the burnin bush and heards the voice of the Lord, "then Moses trembled, and durst not behold".

If John, the one who so trusted in the love and truthfulness of Jesus that him referred to himself as "the one who Jesus loved", fell at the Lord Jesus' feet like a dead man at the sight of hims glory, who are we to thinks we cans stand in hims presence in our own goodness? If the prophets Ezekiel and Daniel couldn't stand on theirs feet before the glory of the Lord and the glory of hims angel, how cans we? Moses weres chosen to deliver the nation of Israel from all the power and might of Egypt, yet him trembled at the voice of God. We can't expect to stand before a righteous judge in our own works and on our own merits. If the Apostle John or Moses couldn't stand before him, how cans we? Haves any of us done miracles like they dids? Haves any of us personally lived and worked alongside Jesus like John dids? Haves any of us beens brave enough or loved the Lord enough to risk our very lives for him? If John weres speechless at the sight of hims Lord and Savior, I cans assure you we are not goin to be able to say one word in our own defense. When we looks a holy God in the eye someday we will be aware of just how righteous him is, and just how unrighteous we are, and we won't say a word because in that moment we will know that any judgment him passes on us be justified. When I looks my humans in the eyes after doin somethin I knows is wrong, I also knows their withholdin of treats or reward is justified. There is no need for me to try and makes excuses because I knows that they are right.

The judge also is a father, and God loves all humans like a good father loves hims children. So in order to keep from passin judgment on humans, God needed a sacrifice that weres so perfect and holy that it woulds be enough to justify every one of you once and for all time. Him couldn't be righteous without judgin, but him didn't want to pass sentence on anyone because of hims love, so him hads no other way to save mankind than to send hims own son in the flesh to take the punishment for everyone. The most amazin thing bouts this is that him would haves done this even if only one person needed him, the same as an earthly father woulds be willin to die if it woulds save the life of only one of hims children. So you see, it weren't because the whole human race weres in danger that Jesus offered himself in your place. Him weres willin to die for just one of hims children, or all of hims children, just like any good father.

Maybe some of you didn't have a good earthly father. Maybe it's difficult to imagine what a good father woulds even be like. Let's think bouts this for a minute. Wouldn't all of us like to be loved by someone so much that they woulds be willin to risk theirs life for us? Doesn't we all think the image of a good father woulds be a man who woulds give up hims life to save hims child? It seems to me a good father puts the needs of hims children ahead of hims own needs. This is the kind of father God is! I finds this so excitin and wonderful. If you didn't have a good earthly father then you are in for an extraordinary new life gettin to know your heavenly father through Christ Jesus.

Jesus saids in John 14:6 that no man comes to the Father except through him. Hims offer is all-inclusive and hims invitation is extended to every human on the face of the earth. Him doesn't discriminate. You cans be any nationality, any color, male or female. You cans be a person who haves lived a pretty moral life or a person who feels you haves lived a terrible mistake-filled life. Jesus just says come to him. Him is perfectly able to make any changes that needs to be mades after you gets there, but him turns nobody away. Him says in John 6:37b, "And him that cometh to me I will in no wise cast out."

There are no resumes to submit, no applications to fill out, no background checks, no drug tests, no interviews, no criteria to meet. Jesus just says come to him the way you are right now and him won't turn anybody away. Him is able to handle your past and him is able to gives you a better future. I doesn't know anybody else who loves the way him loves. It's so simple even a little doggie like me cans understand it and stand in awe of the simplicity and power of this plan. As we wraps up the main course of our dinner I can't help but think what a wonderful God him is to invite everyone to sit down at hims table. Him doesn't care if you wears your finest clothes or if all you haves to wear is rags. Him loves everyone alike. Every person is beautiful, valuable, and worthy of love in hims eyes. What a great father him is!

# STRENGTH, SONG, SALVATION

*"The Lord is my strength and song, and is become my salvation."*
PSALM 118:14

MAYBE AT THIS POINT you are feelin like you wants to know more bouts this Jesus. You mights be thinkin you woulds love to haves the peace in your heart that comes from a relationship with him. It sure is nice to lie down at night and not haves to worry over the weight of sins, or what is gonna happen once this life here on earth is over. If you are thinkin any of these things, I am goin to tells you how you cans have this special relationship that is like no other. This is God's promise to us bouts the Lord Jesus in Hebrews 7:25, "Wherefore he is able also to save them to the uttermost that come unto God by him, seeing he ever liveth to make intercession for them."

We haves arrived at the dessert portion of our meal at the Master's table. I knows of no sweeter person than the Lord Jesus Christ. If you ever wondered what God is really like all you has to do is look at Jesus. Hims love and compassion and entire personality are God in the flesh. Him didn't haves to come here to save humankind from weaknesses and sins but him dids it willinly out of love. In a moment you will be able to follow a prayer to ask Jesus into your life and in that moment you will be set free of all the things you ever dids wrong. This whole matter will be settled forever in heaven that you belongs to the Lord and are a new person. The Apostle Paul says this bouts salvation in 2 Corinthians 5:17, "Therefore if any man be in Christ, he is a new creature: old things are passed away; behold, all things are become new." Generally speakin, in life you doesn't normally gets do-overs but in Jesus Christ you haves the opportunity to start over and begin a fresh new life. Doesn't that sound wonderful? Because of hims sacrifice you are able to begin again with a clean slate. That is the most refreshin idea I ever heards.

If you already haves a relationship with Jesus Christ but woulds just enjoy repeatin the words of the prayer along with us, to honor him and reaffirm your commitment, you are most welcome.

If you doesn't yet feels like you are at the point of prayin the prayer, but are curious bouts Jesus and interested in knowin more, then study all you cans bouts him in the Bible. Everything we needs to know is right there. Jesus saids this bouts himself in John 5:39, "Search the scriptures; for in them ye think ye have eternal life: and they are they which testify of me."

Maybe at this point you still doubts there actually is a God. I woulds like to invite you to ask him to reveal himself to you, to prove himself to be real and lovin and interested in your life. I believes with all my little heart God will answer if you asks with a sincere heart. Will him answer immediately with a voice from the sky or some other dramatic display?

## Strength, Song, Salvation

Well, probably not with an audible voice but I haves heards many stories of folkses who weres seekin to know if God weres real and him answered in unmistakable ways.

I haves asked Mommy to lead the prayer of repentance and salvation because I doesn't thinks you shoulds say the prayer in my doggie voice. You cans follow along word by word or put it into your own words. This is your own private time with the maker of the universe and you shoulds speak to him in whichever way you feels most comfortable. The highest point in our dinner at the Master's table is takin place right now. The Lord himself is servin dessert!

"Dear God,

I come to you because I believe you are the maker of all things. I admit to you that I have failed and fallen short and I have made many mistakes. I confess my sins and faults to you, Lord, and I declare that you are holy.

I believe that Jesus Christ is your son, and that he is God in the flesh. I believe he was born of a virgin, that he lived a holy and sinless life, and that he was crucified for my sins. I believe he rose from the grave as a sign that his sacrifice was acceptable to you, and I believe he forever lives to make intercession for me.

Right now I accept the Lord Jesus Christ into my heart as my personal savior. I ask you to cleanse my heart and forgive me of all my sins. I ask you to guide me with your Holy Spirit and help me to live a life that honors and pleases you.

I am now your child and have become a new person in Jesus. My sins are gone and cast behind your back. I know that you are a forward-looking God and you are not going to look backwards at my sins but forward toward my new life in Christ. I trust you with my life here on earth and with my eternal soul.

Thank you, Lord, for your sacrifice for me. Thank you for forgiving me of my sins. Thank you for saving me to the uttermost.

It is in Jesus' name and for his honor and glory I pray,

Amen"

# TASTE AND SEE

*"O taste and see that the Lord is good: blessed is the man that trusteth in him."*
PSALM 34:8

I HAVES NEVER HADS a tastier meal than the one I just shared with you at the Master's table! I hopes you feels the same way. My heart, mind, soul, and spirit haves beens fed with the goodness of hims truth and love. I haves the strength to go on with my life in a spirit of hope, no matter what tomorrow brings, because my Master is with me. Him loves me and him loves you too. I hopes you feels the love and that you continues to grow in your relationship with him.

Just in case you weres wonderin, this rich meal weren't a one-time thing but we all are invited to sit down at the Master's table every single day. In fact, we needs to eat with him every day. Him will sustain us so we doesn't go out into the world runnin on empty. Not only does the Master invite us daily to eat at hims table, but we cans invite him to come into our own homes and eat with us! We cans invite him into every area of our lives and him is more than happy to oblige. The Lord Jesus himself saids this in Revelation 3:20, "Behold, I stand at the door, and knock: if any man hear my voice, and open the door, I will come in to him, and will sup with him, and he with me."

Cans you imagine any greater honor than knowin the creator of all things wants to come to your house and sit at the table with you? Imagine how honored and excited we woulds feel if some great world ruler called up and asked to come to our house and eat with us. Well, I am sorry to say that's not likely to happen. The rulers of this world are too busy to haves time for little doggies like me or even for regular citizens like you. But the King of kings and Lord of lords, who is far above all rulers and governments, desires more than anything else to sit at the table and spend time with you! The Lord Jesus Christ, the one who mades you and lived for you and died for you and rose from the dead for you, wants to come into your very own home and sit down and eat with you. Him doesn't care whether you has steak on the table or those soup beans and fried taters because all him wants is to spend time in sweet fellowship with you: the folkses him created with hims own hands.

I can't emphasize this privilege and honor enough. Who coulds be greater than God? Yet him loves humans and the whole focus of hims plan since the world began is to reconcile you to himself. Imagine enjoin this good meal every day of your lives!

If you chose to accept Jesus Christ as your savior I invites you to come over to my Facebook page called "Belinda Belle Brewer" to lets me know. Mommy and I and all our sweet friends will pray for you and for your new life in Christ. You haves embarked on the greatest adventure there is and I feels so excited for you and I encourages you to grow every day in your new relationship with Jesus. A good Bible, a good church, and good godly friends will be of great help to you as you starts on this new path. Be sure to sit with the Master at hims table very day. Folkses make many decisions in life and some of them are regrettable, but I haves never once heard anyone say they regretted invitin Jesus into their lives.

If you didn't choose at this time to ask Jesus into your heart, or if you still haves doubts, I wants you to know that I loves you and God loves you. You are also in my prayers and I invites you to keep an open mind bouts God and hims love for you. You are always welcome at hims table.

Keep askin, seekin, and knockin. Keep readin, researchin, and askin God to answer. Him is faithful. Don't give up. Him is on hims way to the table and him wants to linger with you over the best meal you ever hads. If you haves doubts or questions, or if you just wants to sit a while in hims presence, the Master's table is the best place you cans possibly be.

Taste and see that the Lord is good!

27788274R00050

Made in the USA
Charleston, SC
22 March 2014